SPECIAL DAYS

Autumn

Liz Gogerly

W
FRANKLIN WATTS
LONDON • SYDNEY

SPECIAL DAYS

Titles in this series:

Autumn

Spring

Summer

Winter

© 2004 Arcturus Publishing

Produced for Franklin Watts by Arcturus Publishing Ltd, 26/27 Bickels Yard, 151–153 Bermondsey Street, London SE1 3HA.

Series concept: Alex Woolf
Editor: Cath Senker
Designer: Tim Mayer
Picture researcher: Shelley Noronha, Glass Onion Pictures

Published in the UK by Franklin Watts.

A CIP catalogue record for this book is available from the British Library.

ISBN 07496 5459 7

Printed in Italy.

Franklin Watts – the Watts Publishing Group, 96 Leonard Street, London EC2A 4XD.

Picture Acknowledgements:
Andes Picture Agency 21; Al Pix, all credited to Superbild, *cover* (top left), 14, 24; Martyn Chillmaid *cover* (bottom right), 10; Camera Press (Allan Milligan) 5; CIRCA (William Holtby) *cover* (top right), (John Smith) *cover* (bottom left), (Barrie Searle) *cover* (bottom centre) and 13, (John Smith) 22, (William Holtby) 29; Eye Ubiquitous (Chris Fairclough) *cover* (top centre), (John Hulme) *title page*, (Chris Fairclough) 20, (John Hulme) 28; Hutchison (Christine Pemberton) 7; Ann and Bury Peerless 6, 23; David Silverman 9, 12; Topham Picturepoint, all credited to The Image Works except 27, (Kathy McCoughlin) 4, (David Wells) 8, (Michael Schwarz) 11, (Frank Pedrick) 17, (Bob Daemmrich) 19, (Kathy McCoughlin) 26, (Martin Keene) 27; World Religions 15, 16, 18, 25.

Cover pictures (clockwise from left): Id ul-Fitr; Diwali; Kathina; Harvest Festival; Sukkot; Guru Nanak's birthday.

Note:
The quotations in this book are fictionalized accounts drawn from factual sources.

Contents

Note: When Muslims say the name of one of the Prophets, they say 'Peace Be Upon Him' afterwards. This is shown in Arabic as ﷺ in this book.

Autumn Days and Nights

In the **northern hemisphere** it is autumn in September, October and November. In September, it is often warm in the day. At night, it begins to feel chilly and it seems like winter is on its way. In the USA, the first Monday in September is Labor Day. This national holiday marks the end of summer. Many tourist attractions close for the winter.

In autumn, farmers are in their fields gathering fruit and vegetables. Most religions have a festival to celebrate bringing in a good harvest. Christians call theirs Harvest Festival and Jewish people call theirs Sukkot.

Another sign of autumn is the changing colours of the leaves on the trees. They turn to yellow, red, orange and gold. Soon, the leaves tumble from the branches.

As the autumn leaves pile high we have to sweep them up.

Amy's Guy Fawkes Night

'We go to an organized firework display on Guy Fawkes Night. The younger kids make a Guy out of old clothes. It goes on top of the bonfire and we cheer when it catches fire. I like the fireworks that spray different colours everywhere. The bangers are a bit scary because they sound like bombs going off. The best part of the night is the food – yummy hotdogs and burgers!'

Amy, Scunthorpe, UK

On Guy Fawkes Night people in the UK remember when the Houses of Parliament were nearly blown up in a plot against the government.

Autumn festivals can be great fun. At Halloween, people dress up as witches and ghosts. During the Hindu festival of Diwali, fireworks brighten up the dark skies. In the UK, there are bonfires and firework displays on 5 November to celebrate Guy Fawkes Night.

5

Ganesh Chaturthi, August or September

Lord Ganesha, with his elephant head and rounded body, is a popular god in the Hindu religion. He is the god of knowledge and wisdom. Hindus believe that worshipping him will help to bring happiness and success to their lives.

A woman lights candles in front of the shrine of Ganesha.

In August or September, Hindus celebrate Ganesha's birthday. The celebrations last for ten days and begin with families cleaning their homes. They give a *murti* of Ganesha pride of place on their **shrine**. Over the following days, the family and guests place **offerings**, such as flowers or money, in front of Ganesha. They light candles and sing hymns. Afterwards, the family gives out sweets and fruit.

People in the city of Mumbai in India watch as an enormous *murti* of Ganesha is immersed in the river.

The *murti* of Ganesha is usually kept for ten days. On the tenth day, the family gathers for a special ceremony in which the *murti* is thrown into a river, the sea or a well for **immersion**. As Ganesha falls in the water, people sing a song, asking him to come again the following year.

Lalit's Ganesh Chaturthi

'There are big traffic jams on the tenth day of the festival. Families are crammed into their cars, taking the *murtis* of Ganesha to the beach to be immersed in water. There are also lorries going to the beach with the large *murtis* that were put up in the streets and temples. There's noise everywhere – from the tooting cars, drums and gongs. It's an exciting day and one of the biggest beach parties you'll ever see.'
Lalit, Mumbai, India

Rosh Hashanah and Yom Kippur, September or October

Of all Jewish festivals, Rosh Hashanah and Yom Kippur are the most important religious occasions. Most Jews try to visit the **synagogue**, their place of worship, during this holy time.

Rosh Hashanah is the Jewish New Year and is a two-day festival. At the synagogue, people consider their past deeds and the mistakes they have made. The **rabbi** blows the *shofar* (a ram's horn) to call everyone to ask God for forgiveness. At this time, Jewish people also remember how God gave them the Torah, their holy book.

A rabbi blows the *shofar* 100 times at the start of Rosh Hashanah.

Special candles are lit at sundown on the first night of Yom Kippur.

Aaron's Yom Kippur

'I've only just had my *Bar Mitzvah* so this year is the first time I could fast at Yom Kippur. We didn't eat or drink anything for 25 hours – imagine that! It wasn't as hard as I thought it would be, and I really felt part of the Jewish community. This is going to be a great year!'
Aaron, Chicago, USA

At New Year, families usually gather for a festive meal. They start with a sweet food – usually apples dipped in honey. This symbolizes sweetness and hope for the year ahead.

Yom Kippur

Ten days after Rosh Hashanah it is Yom Kippur, the Day of Atonement. It is the holiest day in the Jewish calendar. Many Jews begin a twenty-five hour **fast** at sunset on the eve of Yom Kippur. The next day they pray in the synagogue and ask God to forgive them for their **sins**. The festival ends at sunset when the *shofar* is blown.

9

Harvest Festival, September Thanksgiving, November

During the Christian harvest festival many people make offerings of food in church. This food is often distributed to old people's homes or hostels for the homeless.

Harvest festivals are for giving thanks for the food grown in the summer and harvested in the autumn. The tradition of these festivals goes back a long time. The ancient Greeks honoured Demeter, the goddess of corn, at a special festival each autumn. They gave her **offerings** and then they feasted and danced.

These days, Christians celebrate harvest by decorating their churches. Autumn flowers, fruit and vegetables make a beautiful display. There are special services and people sing hymns giving thanks to God. At this time Christians also think about people in other parts of the world who might be hungry.

Children enjoy decorating their schools at harvest time. They bring fresh produce or other food to school. Often there is a school assembly with hymns and harvest stories. Later, the food the children have collected is boxed up and given to needy people in the local community.

In November each year, Americans head home to celebrate Thanksgiving with their families. Many towns hold street parades and parties. All these festivities are to **commemorate** the first successful harvest gathered by the English settlers in the USA nearly 400 years ago.

At Thanksgiving there is a family meal, and people give cards and presents.

Danny's Thanksgiving

'We all go to my grandparents for Thanksgiving. Grandma cooks the biggest turkey you have ever seen. Her pumpkin pie is the best ever. Before dinner one of the kids always says a prayer saying 'thank you' for the meal we are about to eat. Much later, we play games.'
Danny, Detroit, USA

Sukkot, October

The Jewish festival of Sukkot is great fun for children. They help to make and decorate a *sukkah* (hut). The *sukkah* has at least three sides and a roof that is usually made from branches. Inside, people hang fruit and vegetables. Often they put up decorations, cards and flags to create a festive look. Throughout the week-long festival, families eat their meals in the hut. If they live in a hot climate they might even sleep there.

This custom is a way of remembering when the Jewish people lived in the desert for forty years. They had escaped slavery in Egypt and were waiting to enter the land of Israel. During those long years in the desert they lived in huts. Copying how their people lived long ago helps Jews today to think about their own lives. They feel thankful for their homes and the many things that they own.

These children decorate the *sukkah* with fresh citrus fruits. It is the custom to build the roof so that it's possible to see the sky through the gaps.

Avi's Sukkot

'In synagogue, we wave the *lulav* and *etrog* in all directions to show that God is everywhere. The *lulav* is made from branches of palm, myrtle and willow tree. The *etrog* is a citrus fruit that is grown in Israel – it's like a lemon.'

Avi, Haifa, Israel

At the synagogue the *lulav* is held in the right hand and the *etrog* is held in the left while special songs are sung.

Sukkot also **commemorates** the end of the harvest. By this time of year, the farmers have picked the fruits and gathered in the vegetables. Now is the time to celebrate their hard work and give thanks for a good harvest.

13

Ramadan and Lailat ul-Qadr

The Muslim year is shorter than the Western calendar year. Muslim festivals take place on the same date each year in the Muslim calendar, but change according to the Western calendar.

Ramadan starts in the ninth month of the Muslim calendar. This was the month that the Muslim holy book, the *Qur'an*, was revealed to the Prophet Muhammad ﷺ. It begins and ends with the birth of a new moon and lasts for twenty-nine or thirty days.

A Saudi Arabian family breaking the fast at Ramadan with a light meal.

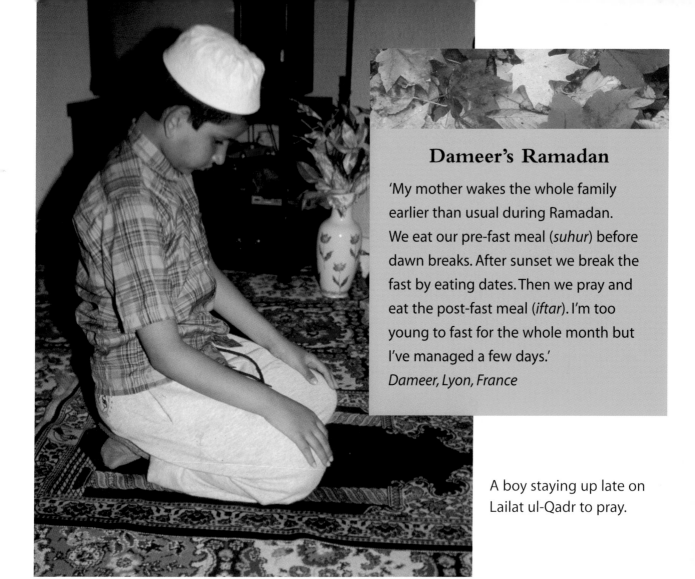

Dameer's Ramadan

'My mother wakes the whole family earlier than usual during Ramadan. We eat our pre-fast meal (*suhur*) before dawn breaks. After sunset we break the fast by eating dates. Then we pray and eat the post-fast meal (*iftar*). I'm too young to fast for the whole month but I've managed a few days.'
Dameer, Lyon, France

A boy staying up late on Lailat ul-Qadr to pray.

For Muslims all around the world, Ramadan is a time for reflection and prayer. People aged twelve or over **fast** during daylight hours. This helps them to concentrate on prayer and feel closer to Allah (God). During the month they try to read as much of the *Qur'an* as possible. Some people even read all of it.

Lailat ul-Qadr

Lailat ul-Qadr is the Night of Power, which takes place in the last ten days of Ramadan. It is the anniversary of the very first night that the *Qur'an* was revealed to Muhammad ﷺ. Towns are often lit up with bright lights in celebration. Many Muslims stay up all night praying.

Halloween 31 October

By the end of October, the days seem much shorter. Few people like the longer evenings, but a dark night is perfect for celebrating Halloween.

On 31 October every year, there is fun and mischief in the air. People dress up as ghosts, vampires, witches and skeletons. Sometimes they go to fancy-dress parties – the person with the best costume wins a prize! There are games such as **apple bobbing**.

In the USA and UK, children visit their neighbours and play 'trick or treat'. If they are not given sweets or another treat, then they play a trick on the neighbour. Another Halloween custom is making lanterns from hollowed-out pumpkins.

Dressing up at Halloween is great fun. People wear scary outfits and masks.

Making carved-out pumpkins , called Jack O'Lanterns, is another custom at Halloween.

Halloween dates back to ancient times. In parts of the UK and France the Celtic people believed that the evening of 31 October marked the end of the year and the beginning of winter. They lit bonfires to chase away evil spirits. The word 'Halloween' comes from 'Hallowmas', another word for the Christian All Saints' Day, which takes place on 1 November. Eventually, the night before All Saints' Day was called All Hallows Eve. Then it became Halloween.

Keomi's Halloween

'In China, the Halloween festival is called Teng Chieh. We put out food and water in front of photographs of people in our family who have died. We also light lanterns and bonfires. This is to guide the **spirits** as they travel on earth on the night of Halloween .'
Keomi, London, UK

Days of the Dead, November

Towards the end of October, shops throughout Mexico are filled with skulls and skeletons. They are made from wood, plastic or clay – or even sugar and chocolate so they can be eaten! The skeletons are dressed in all kinds of costumes, anything from football players to doctors. All these skeletons play a big part in the customs of the Mexican Days of the Dead.

On 1–2 November, Mexican people **commemorate** the life and death of their loved ones. They believe that on these days, the **spirits** of the dead visit home. They use the skeletons to decorate small **altars** or graves dedicated to their loved ones who have died. People also cover the graves in streamers and flowers.

Mexican people do not find skulls and skeletons frightening. The Days of the Dead are a time for fun and joyous celebrations.

A family decorates the grave of their loved one with bright flowers, ribbons and flags.

Angelito's Day of the Dead

'When he was alive my grandpa liked to fish. So on 2 November we bring a model of a skeleton fishing and place it on his grave. He also loved chocolate and bananas so we take those along too. By putting these things on his grave he knows that he's come back to the right place and that he's very welcome.'

Angelito, Mexico City, Mexico

On 1 November people remember lost children, and on 2 November they honour dead adults. On both days, families go to graveyards with picnics and drink to toast the dead. Some people bring along musical instruments and sing. At dusk, people light candles and sometimes there are fireworks. The graveside parties often last all night.

19

Diwali, October or November

A Hindu woman lights incense and candles in front of an image of Lakshmi, the goddess of wealth.

Diwali, the Hindu Festival of Light, lasts for five days. In the northern hemisphere, it is celebrated as the nights draw in and become long and cold. At Diwali, Hindus remember their gods; people from each area of India have their own favourites.

On the first day of Diwali, Hindu families clean their homes and open up the windows to let in Lakshmi, the goddess of wealth. By placing flowers everywhere they hope to please the goddess. To welcome her on her way, they light rows of candles.

The third day of Diwali is the last day of the Hindu year. At night, homes and temples (where people worship) are lit up with coloured lights, lanterns or rows of oil lamps. Hindus believe that light helps us to see the beauty of this world. They also see light as the triumph of good over evil and of happiness over sadness.

The following day is the Hindu New Year. People head to the temples to take part in special services. Families usually get together to eat a special meal. Often they exchange gifts, such as sweets and clothes. Afterwards, they whoop and cheer at the firecrackers and fireworks.

Nidra's Diwali

'I save up to buy my own sparklers and *phatakas* (firecrackers) for Diwali. My dad says that the noise of the fireworks is to chase away evil spirits. When the fireworks make a loud bang I think about all the good luck we are bringing into the New Year.'

Nidra, Colombes, France

This girl wears her finest clothes for dancing at a Diwali celebration.

Guru Nanak's birthday, October or November

Many Sikh festivals are anniversaries of the births and deaths of the Sikh **Gurus**. These are called *gurpurbs*. The first **Guru** and founder of Sikhism was Guru Nanak. The anniversary of his birthday is one of the most important *gurpurbs*.

A crowd of people watches as a float with the Guru Granth Sahib on board is paraded at the festival in Anandapur, India.

Guru Nanak was born in India in 1469. In those days, most people in India were either Muslim or Hindu. Guru Nanak founded a new religion. He taught that all people were equal in God's eyes, and that they should serve God by praying, working hard and helping others.

22

Sikhs having fun at the fair that is held as part of the festival.

Birthday celebrations begin by reading the holy book, the Guru Granth Sahib, from beginning to end. This is called *akhand path*. People take turns – it takes 48 hours altogether! On the third day of the festival there is often a procession and the Guru Granth Sahib is paraded on a float.

Veerinda's celebrations

'The celebrations are massive here. In the grand procession, there are bands playing and people singing everywhere. I really like watching the swordsmen perform – they are so cool. Every year the Golden Temple is lit up with millions of little oil lamps. It looks magical, like a beautiful floating palace.'
Veerinda, Amritsar, India

Heading the procession are five men who represent the first five members of the Sikh community. They lead everyone to the *gurdwara*, the Sikh place of worship. A large crowd follows, singing hymns or reading from the holy book. In the streets, people give out sweets and cold drinks. Later, there is a special meal at the *gurdwara* and sometimes there are fairs and other street entertainment.

23

Id ul-Fitr

Id ul-Fitr is a joyous festival that celebrates the breaking of the Ramadan **fast** (*see pages 14–15*). At Id, Muslims also celebrate and say thanks for all the good things in their life – such as health, strength and success.

The excitement begins in the last days of Ramadan. Often people buy a whole set of new clothes, including shoes. On the last night of Ramadan, they decorate their homes. The following day, they get up early and put on their best new clothes. Then they visit the mosque, their place of worship, and say special prayers. When they greet their friends and family they say 'Id Mubarak' ('Happy Id').

Afterwards, families gather and eat together. It is the custom to give money to children at Id. Many children spend some of the money at the fairs that are set up specially for the occasion.

It has become the custom to send cards to one another during Id. These Muslim girls made their own cards at school.

After prayers at the mosque, people greet each other warmly.

An important part of Id is giving to charity. Each member of the family contributes a small amount of money to their mosque. This money is then given to poor people to help them celebrate too.

Faizah's Id ul-Fitr

'Id is like our version of Christmas. We send family and friends special cards wishing them a Happy Id. My mother makes up big trays of sweets and cakes. Loads of neighbours and relatives call round and we eat the treats with tea and coffee. It's more traditional to give kids money at Id but sometimes people buy us sweets and toys.'
Faizah, Toronto, Canada

25

Remembrance Day, 11 November

An ex-army officer attends a Veteran's Day Parade in New York, USA.

Remembrance Day is a sad day on which people in many countries remember the **servicemen** and women who have died or been injured fighting in the wars of the last hundred years.

The first Remembrance Day was held the year after the end of the First World War (1914–18). During the war, millions of people were killed or badly injured. The war ended at 11 a.m. on 11 November 1918 – the eleventh hour of the eleventh day of the eleventh month.

After the war, people wanted to remember those who had died and help the survivors. People raised money to help the injured by selling paper poppies. The date 11 November became Remembrance Day, a day to honour the dead.

The nearest Sunday to Remembrance Day is called Remembrance Sunday. On this occasion, people attend special church services. At 11 a.m., they observe a two-minute silence to remember the dead. Later, there are often street parades and people who have fought in wars lay **wreaths** of poppies or crosses on war **memorials**.

Sam's Remembrance Sunday

'At school there are always poppies for sale in the weeks before Remembrance Day. My teacher says that we wear poppies because they grew in the fields of Belgium and France where the soldiers died during the First World War. Remembrance Day makes you think hard about war. Even though we don't know the people who died we still feel sad – war seems such a horrible waste of life.'

Sam, Kingston, Jamaica

An ex-soldier places a cross in memory of a lost friend on a war memorial, UK.

Kathina, October or November

Kathina is a Buddhist festival that is particularly important in Thailand, Sri Lanka and Burma. It's a special time when ordinary people can show appreciation to Buddhist monks and nuns for the work they have done all year.

Each year, Buddhist monks and nuns go on **retreat** during the **monsoon**, the rainy season. Usually, part of a monk's life is to travel between **monasteries** and teach in the community. During the monsoon, the monks cannot travel so they stay in one monastery. They pass the days in **meditation** or study. Kathina falls at the end of the retreat. It's a time of change when many monks move on to a new monastery.

A procession of people in north-east Thailand take their offerings and their gift of cloth to the local monastery.

Dhiman's Kathina

'Each year we take about three metres of cloth to the monastery. This is enough to make one of the main robes. Once the cloth-giving ceremony is over, everybody helps to make the new robe. It is the custom to finish sewing the robe before dawn the following day.'
Dhiman, Pegu, Burma

The cloth will be dyed orange before it is made into robes.

The most important ritual during Kathina is the local people giving cloth to the monastery. This cloth is used to make new robes. People also give useful gifts such as tools or wood to the monks and nuns, who own just a few very basic things. By giving their **offerings** to the monastery, the community is able to give thanks to them. After a special cloth-giving ceremony, the local people and the monks and nuns share a meal together.

Calendar of Festivals

Most religions follow a lunar calendar, based on the moon's movements, rather than a solar calendar. They adjust the calendar to keep the festivals in their season. Muslims don't adjust their calendar, so the festivals can be at any time of the year and are not related to the seasons. Sikh festivals are usually three days long because they include the two-day reading of the Sikh holy book before the festival day. There are no fixed dates for Harvest Festival or Kathina. At the time of going to press there were no dates available for Guru Nanak's birthday in 2005 and 2006.

2004

Labor Day	6 September
Rosh Hashanah	16–17 September
Ganesh Chaturthi	18 September
Yom Kippur	25 September
Sukkot	30 September–6 October
Ramadan	15 October (Ramadan begins)
Halloween	31 October
Days of the Dead	1–2 November
Guy Fawkes Night	5 November
Lailat ul-Qadr	10 November
Remembrance Day	11 November
Diwali	12 November
Id ul-Fitr	14 November
Thanksgiving	25 November
Birthday of Guru Nanak	26 November

2005

Labor Day	5 September
Ganesh Chaturthi	7 September
Ramadan	4 October (Ramadan begins)
Rosh Hashanah	4–5 October
Yom Kippur	13 October
Sukkot	18–24 October
Lailat ul-Qadr	30 October
Halloween	31 October
Diwali	1 November
Days of the Dead	1–2 November
Id ul-Fitr	3 November
Guy Fawkes Night	5 November
Remembrance Day	11 November
Thanksgiving	24 November

2006

Ganesh Chaturthi	27 August
Labor Day	4 September
Rosh Hashanah	22–23 September
Ramadan	24 September (Ramadan begins)
Yom Kippur	2 October
Sukkot	7–13 October
Lailat ul-Qadr	20 October
Diwali	21 October
Id ul-Fitr	24 October
Halloween	31 October
Days of the Dead	1–2 November
Guy Fawkes Night	5 November
Remembrance Day	11 November
Thanksgiving	23 November

Glossary

altars Large tables in temples or churches, used for religious ceremonies.

apple bobbing A game in which people have to catch an apple floating in a bowl of water using only their teeth.

Bar Mitzvah At the age of thirteen, a Jewish boy joins the community as an adult. In a special ceremony he becomes *Bar Mitzvah* ('son of the commandment').

commemorate To do something special to remember an important person or event.

fast To give up eating food, or certain foods, for a time, often for religious reasons.

Guru A Buddist or Sikh teacher.

immersion A religious ceremony in which an object or person is covered in water.

meditation A Buddhist practice: sitting quietly and still in order to become calm, happy and wise.

memorial A place, an object or a custom that is set up to help people remember a person or event.

monasteries The buildings where monks live.

monsoon A period of heavy rain in summer in South Asian countries.

murti Means 'form'. An image or statue of a god or goddess, which is used by Hindus in worship.

northern hemisphere The half of the earth north of the imaginary line around the middle of the earth called the Equator.

offerings Things that are offered in thanks to a god or Prophet.

rabbi A Jewish religious teacher and leader.

retreat Time spent alone or in a quiet place where people can think and meditate.

servicemen People who serve in the army, navy or airforce.

shrine A holy building or place that is set aside for the worship of a god, saint or other holy person.

sins Bad deeds or bad behaviour that goes against religious laws.

spirits Beings without real bodies.

wreaths Arrangements of flowers that are usually placed on memorials or graves in memory of the dead.

Further Information

Books for Children

Celebration: Festivals from Around the World (Children Just Like Me) by Barnabas Kindersley (Dorling Kindersley, 1997)

Festivals Through the Year: Spring by Anita Ganeri (Heinemann Library, 1999)

The Kingfisher Book of Religions: Festivals, Ceremonies and Beliefs from Around the World by T. Barnes (Kingfisher, 1999)

My Buddhist Year, My Hindu Year, My Muslim Year, My Sikh Year, all by Cath Senker (Hodder Wayland, 2003)

My Christian Year and My Jewish Year, both by Cath Senker (Hodder Wayland, 2002)

My Life as a Christian, My Life as a Hindu, My Life as a Jew, My Life as a Muslim, My Life as a Sikh by Trevor Guy, Sue Mizon, Paul Morgan (Dref Wen, 1999)

Websites

www.theresite.org.uk/

UK site with RE resources and links.

http://website.lineone.net/~jlancs/reintro.htm

Schoolchildren from Frenchwood school talk about their religions, including festivals: Hindu, Muslim, Buddhist and Christian faiths.

Index

All numbers in **bold** refer to pictures as well as text.